Francis Frith's
Gloucestershire

Photographic Memories

Francis Frith's
Gloucestershire

Keith Howell

FRITH
BOOK Co

First published in the United Kingdom in 2000 by
Frith Book Company Ltd

Text and Design copyright © Frith Book Company Ltd
Photographs copyright © The Francis Frith Collection

The Frith photographs and the Frith logo are reproduced under licence from
Heritage Photographic Resources Ltd, the owners of the Frith archive and trademarks

British Library Cataloguing in Publication Data

Francis Frith's Gloucestershire
Keith Howell
ISBN 1-85937-102-7

Frith Book Company Ltd
Frith's Barn, Teffont,
Salisbury, Wiltshire SP3 5QP
Tel: +44 (0) 1722 716 376
Email: info@frithbook.co.uk
www.frithbook.co.uk

Printed and bound in Great Britain

Front Cover: Birdlip, The George Hotel 1907 59062

Contents

Francis Frith: Victorian Pioneer   7

Frith's Archive - A Unique Legacy   10

Gloucestershire - an Introduction   12

Cheltenham and its Environs   14

Eastern Gloucestershire   30

Cirencester and its Environs   38

Gloucester and its Environs   56

Stroud and the Vale of Berkeley   66

The Severn Valley and the Vale of Leadon   96

Index   115

Free Mounted Print Voucher   119

Francis Frith: *Victorian Pioneer*

FRANCIS FRITH, Victorian founder of the world-famous photographic archive, was a complex and multi-talented man. A devout Quaker and a highly successful Victorian businessman, he was both philosophic by nature and pioneering in outlook.

By 1855 Francis Frith had already established a wholesale grocery business in Liverpool, and sold it for the astonishing sum of £200,000, which is the equivalent today of over £15,000,000. Now a multi-millionaire, he was able to indulge his passion for travel. As a child he had pored over travel books written by early explorers, and his fancy and imagination had been stirred by family holidays to the sublime mountain regions of Wales and Scotland. 'What a land of spirit-stirring and enriching scenes and places!' he had written. He was to return to these scenes of grandeur in later years to 'recapture the thousands of vivid and tender memories', but with a different purpose. Now in his thirties, and captivated by the new science of photography, Frith set out on a series of pioneering journeys to the Nile regions that occupied him from 1856 until 1860.

Intrigue and Adventure

He took with him on his travels a specially-designed wicker carriage that acted as both dark-room and sleeping chamber. These far-flung journeys were packed with intrigue and adventure. In his life story, written when he was sixty-three, Frith tells of being held captive by bandits, and of fighting 'an awful midnight battle to the very point of surrender with a deadly pack of hungry, wild dogs'. Sporting flowing Arab costume, Frith arrived at Akaba by camel seventy years before Lawrence, where he encountered 'desert princes and rival sheikhs, blazing with jewel-hilted swords'.

During these extraordinary adventures he was assiduously exploring the desert regions bordering the Nile and patiently recording the antiquities and peoples with his camera. He was the first photographer to venture beyond the sixth cataract. Africa was still the mysterious 'Dark Continent', and Stanley and Livingstone's historic meeting was a decade into the future. The conditions for picture taking confound belief. He laboured for hours in his wicker dark-room in the sweltering heat of the desert, while the volatile chemicals fizzed dangerously in their trays. Often he was forced to work in remote tombs and caves where conditions were cooler. Back in London he exhibited his photographs and was 'rapturously cheered' by members of the Royal Society. His reputation as a photographer was made overnight. An eminent modern historian has likened their impact on the population of the time to that on our own generation of the first photographs taken on the surface of the moon.

Venture of a Life-Time

Characteristically, Frith quickly spotted the opportunity to create a new business as a specialist publisher of photographs. He lived in an era of immense and sometimes violent change. For the poor in the early part of Victoria's reign work was a drudge and the hours long, and people had precious little free time to enjoy themselves. Most had no transport other than a cart or gig at their disposal, and had not travelled far beyond the boundaries of their own town or village. However, by the 1870s, the railways had threaded their way across the country, and Bank Holidays and half-day Saturdays had been made obligatory by Act of Parliament. All of a sudden the ordinary working man and his family were able to enjoy days out and see a little more of the world.

With characteristic business acumen, Francis Frith foresaw that these new tourists would enjoy having souvenirs to commemorate their days out. In 1860 he married Mary Ann Rosling and set out with the intention of photographing every city, town and village in Britain. For the next thirty years he travelled the country by train and by pony and trap, producing fine photographs of seaside resorts and beauty spots that were keenly bought by millions of Victorians. These prints were painstakingly pasted into family albums and pored over during the dark nights of winter, rekindling precious memories of summer excursions.

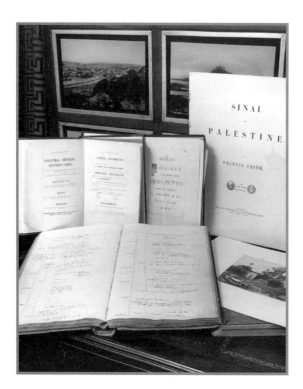

The Rise of Frith & Co

Frith's studio was soon supplying retail shops all over the country. To meet the demand he gathered about him a small team of photographers, and published the work of independent artist-photographers of the calibre of Roger Fenton and Francis Bedford. In order to gain some understanding of the scale of Frith's business one only has to look at the catalogue issued by Frith & Co in 1886: it runs to some 670 pages, listing not only many thousands of views of the British Isles but also many photographs of most European countries, and China, Japan, the USA and

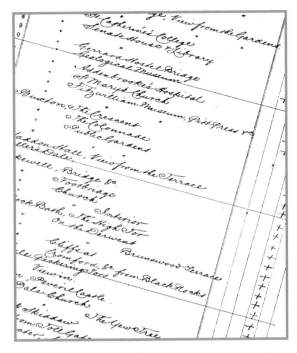

1895 a new size of postcard was permitted called the court card, but there was little room for illustration. In 1899, a year after Frith's death, a new card measuring 5.5 x 3.5 inches became the standard format, but it was not until 1902 that the divided back came into being, with address and message on one face and a full-size illustration on the other. *Frith & Co* were in the vanguard of postcard development, and Frith's sons Eustace and Cyril continued their father's monumental task, expanding the number of views offered to the public and recording more and more places in Britain, as the coasts and countryside were opened up to mass travel.

Francis Frith died in 1898 at his villa in Cannes, his great project still growing. The archive he created continued in business for another seventy years. By 1970 it contained over a third of a million pictures of 7,000 cities, towns and villages. The massive photographic record Frith has left to us stands as a living monument to a special and very remarkable man.

Canada – note the sample page shown above from the hand-written *Frith & Co* ledgers detailing pictures taken. By 1890 Frith had created the greatest specialist photographic publishing company in the world, with over 2,000 outlets – more than the combined number that Boots and W H Smith have today! The picture on the right shows the *Frith & Co* display board at Ingleton in the Yorkshire Dales. Beautifully constructed with mahogany frame and gilt inserts, it could display up to a dozen local scenes.

Postcard Bonanza

The ever-popular holiday postcard we know today took many years to develop. In 1870 the Post Office issued the first plain cards, with a pre-printed stamp on one face. In 1894 they allowed other publishers' cards to be sent through the mail with an attached adhesive halfpenny stamp. Demand grew rapidly, and in

Frith's Archive: *A Unique Legacy*

FRANCIS FRITH'S legacy to us today is of immense significance and value, for the magnificent archive of evocative photographs he created provides a unique record of change in 7,000 cities, towns and villages throughout Britain over a century and more. Frith and his fellow studio photographers revisited locations many times down the years to update their views, compiling for us an enthralling and colourful pageant of British life and character.

We tend to think of Frith's sepia views of Britain as nostalgic, for most of us use them to conjure up memories of places in our own lives with which we have family associations. It often makes us forget that to Francis Frith they were records of daily life as it was actually being lived in the cities, towns and villages of his day. The Victorian age was one of great and often bewildering change for ordinary people, and though the pictures evoke an impression of slower times, life was as busy and hectic as it is today.

We are fortunate that Frith was a photographer of the people, dedicated to recording the minutiae of everyday life. For it is this sheer wealth of visual data, the painstaking chronicle of changes in dress, transport, street layouts, buildings, housing, engineering and landscape that captivates us so much today. His remarkable images offer us a powerful link with the past and with the lives of our ancestors.

Today's Technology

Computers have now made it possible for Frith's many thousands of images to be accessed almost instantly. In the Frith archive today, each photograph is carefully 'digitised' then stored on a CD Rom. Frith archivists can locate a single photograph amongst thousands within seconds. Views can be catalogued and sorted under a variety of categories of place and content to the immediate benefit of researchers.

Inexpensive reference prints can be created for them at the touch of a mouse button, and a wide range of books and other printed materials assembled and published for a wider, more general readership - in the next twelve months over a hundred Frith local history titles will be published! The day-to-day workings of the archive are very different from how they were in Francis Frith's time: imagine the herculean task of sorting through eleven tons of glass negatives as Frith had to do to locate a particular

See Frith at www.frithbook.co.uk

sequence of pictures! Yet the archive still prides itself on maintaining the same high standards of excellence laid down by Francis Frith, including the painstaking cataloguing and indexing of every view.

It is curious to reflect on how the internet now allows researchers in America and elsewhere greater instant access to the archive than Frith himself ever enjoyed. Many thousands of individual views can be called up on screen within seconds on one of the Frith internet sites, enabling people living continents away to revisit the streets of their ancestral home town, or view places in Britain where they have enjoyed holidays. Many overseas researchers welcome the chance to view special theme selections, such as transport, sports, costume and ancient monuments.

We are certain that Francis Frith would have heartily approved of these modern developments in imaging techniques, for he himself was always working at the very limits of Victorian photographic technology.

The Value of the Archive Today

Because of the benefits brought by the computer, Frith's images are increasingly studied by social historians, by researchers into genealogy and ancestory, by architects, town planners, and by teachers and schoolchildren involved in local history projects.

In addition, the archive offers every one of us an opportunity to examine the places where we and our families have lived and worked down the years. Highly successful in Frith's own era, the archive is now, a century and more on, entering a new phase of popularity.

The Past in Tune with the Future

Historians consider the Francis Frith Collection to be of prime national importance. It is the only archive of its kind remaining in private ownership and has been valued at a million pounds. However, this figure is now rapidly increasing as digital technology enables more and more people around the world to enjoy its benefits.

Francis Frith's archive is now housed in an historic timber barn in the beautiful village of Teffont in Wiltshire. Its founder would not recognize the archive office as it is today. In place of the many thousands of dusty boxes containing glass plate negatives and an all-pervading odour of photographic chemicals, there are now ranks of computer screens. He would be amazed to watch his images travelling round the world at unimaginable speeds through network and internet lines.

The archive's future is both bright and exciting. Francis Frith, with his unshakeable belief in making photographs available to the greatest number of people, would undoubtedly approve of what is being done today with his lifetime's work. His photographs, depicting our shared past, are now bringing pleasure and enlightenment to millions around the world a century and more after his death.

Gloucestershire - *An Introduction*

THE FIFTEENTH LARGEST county in England, Gloucestershire's eight hundred thousand acres offer some of the most varied and splendid scenery in Britain. Topographically, it falls naturally into three divisions: the Cotswolds, the Severn Valley and the Royal Forest of Dean Hills, with these areas differing to a surprising degree not only in their geological structure but also in their architecture, flora and climate. Its original boundaries gave it an irregular outline, particularly on the eastern flank, and the Local Government Act of 1972, which transferred part of its southern territory into the new county of Avon, has further complicated this lack of shape, but within its one thousand and thirty square miles lie a host of delightful visual glories, many of which are captured in this collection of photographs by Francis Frith and his associates.

Approached from Oxfordshire in the east, the Cotswold range of rolling Oolitic limestone hills, bisected by rivers, rises gently towards its escarpment above the valley of the River Severn, measuring more than fifty miles from north-east to south-west and attaining a height of more than a thousand feet above sea-level. This bedrock has furnished its inhabitants with an apparently limitless quantity of building stone, in a variety of colours ranging from pale grey to golden-brown, and has contributed immeasurably to the architectural attractions of the region. The Severn Vale, in contrast, is one of lush, green pastures with thatched black-and-white buildings replacing the stone cottages. Across the broad river, the Royal Forest of Dean is a more mysterious area; a mixture of open land and twenty-four thousand tree-covered acres which became England's first

National Forest Park in 1938, and one which also has an industrial past where iron and coal were both mined.

The known history of the region can be traced back to pre-historic times some eighty thousand years ago, and encompasses both Old and New Stone Age people, Bronze Age inhabitants and Iron Age men who all left their mark on this area, and whose dwelling and burial sites have been excavated by archaeologists. The old local saying "scratch Gloucestershire and find Rome" contains more than an element of truth, and there is much evidence of Romano-British civilisation during nearly four centuries of occupation, and the subsequent arrival of the Saxons and Danes prior to the Norman Conquest. By that time, the area's importance was such that Gloucester might well have become the English capital, had not the Normans transferred power to London and the south-east of the country.

The title of Gloucestershire itself first appeared in written records around 1016, and was derived from the name of the county town which, in turn, had come from the Celtic description Caer Glow, "the splendid or beautiful city". But, like numerous other major towns and cities across England, the vandalism and ravages perpetrated by local planning authorities on its venerable streets and buildings in the middle of the last century, make one doubt whether Gloucester's current profile would still generate such a gracious accolade, with only its magnificent cathedral left unmolested to bear witness to its past glories.

Nevertheless, it was during the great wool boom of the 14th and 15th centuries, that the county enjoyed a lengthy period of unparalleled prosperity and the foundations of its present rich architectural heritage were created. The rich cloth merchants bestowed a substantial proportion of their wealth on the building and adornment of the numerous wool churches which still stand across the region, providing the county with a greater architectural panorama than its East Anglian counterparts, which also prospered during this period. These magnificent edifices, along with the stately manor houses and more humble cottages and homes and the verdant surrounding countryside, made Frith's task of scenic photography a relatively simple one. With so many beautiful vistas to choose from, it must have been difficult to decide where to point the camera lens. In the pages of this volume are a selection of the most pleasing, and an encapsulation of Gloucestershire's history over the past hundred years or so. With contemporary pressures and the rapid advance of technological change making themselves increasingly felt in our twenty-first century mode of living, it is gratifying to discover that so much of Gloucestershire's heritage remains for us to enjoy and savour.

Cheltenham & its Environs

Cheltenham, The College Playing Fields 1907 59038

Deerhurst, Wightfield Manor 1901 47309
The walls of this early 16th-century house are partially built with stone taken from a chapel at the monastery at nearby Deerhurst in around 1547, following the Dissolution. The Cassey family lived here until around 1670; their griffin head emblem and a number of Tudor mullioned windows still survive, along with interior 17th-century panelling.

▼ Tewkesbury, Mythe Bridge 1891 29360A

This is Thomas Telford's iron bridge, crossing the River Severn at its junction with the River Avon. Constructed in 1826, and with a single arched span of a hundred and seventy six feet, it was considered an engineering marvel at the time of its completion. On the extreme left is the small tollhouse at the bridge's eastern approach.

▼ Tewkesbury, The Abbey 1893 32102

One of the country's largest parish churches, the abbey was founded in the 8th century, and refounded in 1091. Its great Norman tower is 132 feet high and 46 feet square, and dates from 1150. The Benedictine Abbey of Tewkesbury was the last of the monasteries to be dissolved by Henry VIII, and was saved from destruction by the townspeople buying it from the king for £453 in January 1539.

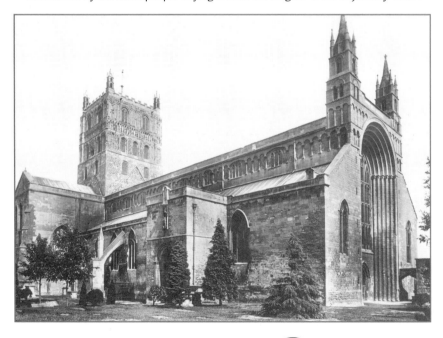

▲ Tewkesbury, Church Street 1907 59072

The 18th-century Royal Hop Pole Hotel on the right-hand side of the street, with its wrought iron, flower-bedecked canopy and window boxes, is featured in Charles Dickens's 'Pickwick Papers', when Pickwick and his three companions dine there on their way from Bristol to Birmingham; they consume bottled ale, Madeira and four bottles of port. Further along is a 17th-century timber-framed building with a double overhang, whose lintel is dated 1664.

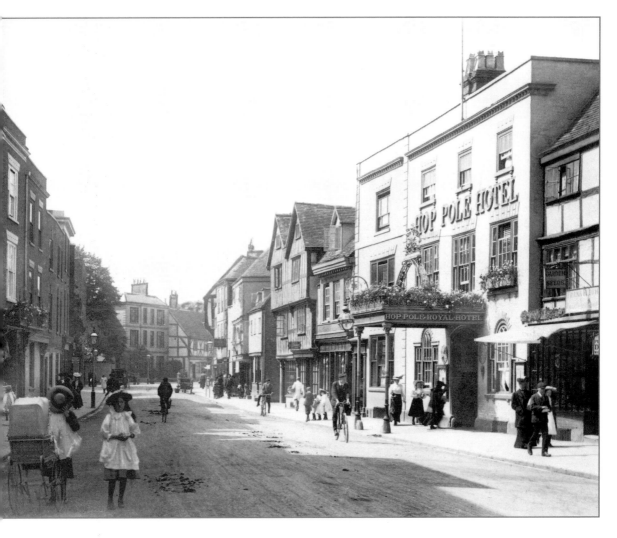

◀ **Tewkesbury, King John's Bridge 1907** 57679
Here we see leisurely recreation on the River Avon in front of King John's Bridge, which was built, according to tradition, by that monarch in 1197. Until the 19th century it was called the Long Bridge; it had undergone extensive repairs in the reign of King Charles I. Beyond is the timber-framed Black Bear inn, which is said to have existed in 1308, but is in fact a much restored 15th-century building.

◄ **Winchcombe**
High Street c1960 W378017
Winchcombe was once the walled capital of Winchcombeshire, whose abbot sat in the Saxon parliament; it was the site of the martyrdom of Kenelm, the child king of the Mercians, who was allegedly killed by his sister Quendrida in AD 819. According to legend, she leaned out of her window and recited psalm 109 backwards; the divine retribution for this deed was that her sight was destroyed. Kenelm's death made his grave second only to Thomas Becket's as a site of pilgrimage during the Middle Ages, and Winchcombe one of the region's earliest tourist centres.

◀ **Tewkesbury, Church Street 1907** 59071
The view of Church Street from the opposite side of the roadway shows the medieval timber frontage of the Berkeley Arms Hotel with its first floor mullioned window, while further along is a four-storied, overhanging 16th-century building and shop. On the near side of the street, parked close to the butcher's and optician's, is a motor vehicle whose registration letters AB 100 mark it as being one of the earliest to take to the road in Britain.

▼ **Cleeve Hill 1907** 59057
The Cotswolds reach their highest point at West Down, 1083 feet above sea level, above this parish of Cleeve Hill, east of Cheltenham. The deep troughs around the summit are caused by slippage of the scarp face, caused by the undermining of the oolitic limestone structure by water pressure. The adjoining common is designated as a site of Special Scientific Interest.

◀ **Southam, Southam Delabere 1901** 47303
One of the largest surviving 16th-century houses in the county, this magnificent house was owned by the de la Bere family until around 1831. It was then bought by Lord Ellenborough, the Governor General of India from 1841-44, who built the semi-detached neo-Norman tower on the east side on his return from India.

◀ **Prestbury, The Village 1901** 47298
Reputedly England's most haunted village, and a market town in the time of Henry III, Prestbury is now a residential suburb of Cheltenham. The record-breaking champion jockey Fred Archer, who was born in Cheltenham in 1857, grew up in the 16th-century half-timbered King's Arms Inn where his father was landlord. He made his first appearance as a rider at the age of eight, when he rode a donkey at a local sports meeting.

Prestbury
The Village 1907 59051
Across the road from the pub is the thatched bakery whose owner, Philip Delaney, presented chocolates to the Queen Mother each year as she passed through on her way to the Cheltenham Race Meeting.

Leckhampton, The Devil's Chimney 1901 47256
This is not a natural rock formation, but one carved out deliberately by the quarrymen extracting building stone, used for the construction of Cheltenham, from this precipitous cliff face. A 19th-century tramway was unofficially used by the public to reach the top of the hill, where some foolhardy visitors climbed this pinnacle, as we can see from these pictures.

Leckhampton
The Devil's Chimney
1901 47257
The practice of climbing the rock is now strictly forbidden, not only on grounds of safety but also to protect the landmark from erosion. Leckhampton Hill, and the surrounding four hundred acres of grassland, were purchased by Cheltenham Town Council in 1929, and the area is now designated as a Site of Special Scientific Interest.

Cheltenham, The Promenade 1901 47260
Cheltenham's Promenade is shaded by horse-chestnut trees, and its elegance at the turn of the century is clearly apparent, with a uniformed coachman patiently awaiting the return of his passengers; they are possibly being groomed inside Ursell's hairdressing and perfumery shop.

Cheltenham, The Winter Gardens 1901 47258
The majestic Winter Gardens building, a smaller imitation of the Crystal Palace, was demolished during the Second World War; it stood at the end of the tree-lined Promenade. The two large cannon, on the right, being admired by a small boy, were captured at Sebastopol during the Crimean War.

Cheltenham, The Promenade 1901 47261
The broad tree-lined Promenade is lined with elegant houses, whose delicate and graceful wrought- and cast-iron work on the balconies and verandas has long been particularly admired. The eastern side of the street was mainly occupied by shops, while the opposite side was mainly made up of offices, both municipal and business.

Cheltenham, The Upper Promenade 1907 59034
This was built in 1823; according to Pevsner, it is 'a great terrace, equal to any in Europe'. In 1916 the central seven houses were converted into Municipal Offices, and these were further extended to other houses in the terrace after the Second World War. The Imperial Rooms, where the British Medical Association held their meeting in 1901, had originally been the Imperial Spa, and this building was demolished to make way for a cinema.

Cheltenham, The Upper Promenade 1901 47263

Cheltenham, The Upper Promenade 1901 47264

▼ Cheltenham, The Pittville Pump Room 1901 47295

The lawyer Joseph Pitt, Rector and MP, amassed a fortune which he used to develop the Pittville area of Cheltenham in the mid 1820s. He laid out gardens and a lake over some eighteen acres at a cost of nearly half a million pounds, although the scheme was not entirely completed for financial reasons. The Pump Room, built by John Forbes in 1825, was modelled on engravings of the Temple of Ilissus in Athens. The alkaline saline waters from the mineral springs can still be taken there, and the building, with its three prominent statues of Aesculapius, Hygeia and Hippocrates, now also houses a museum and is used for concerts.

▼ Cheltenham, The Ladies' College 1906 54324

The prospectus for this famous educational establishment offering 'a College for the education of young ladies and children under eight' was drawn up in 1853, and the school opened the following year at Cambray House. In 1873, the school moved to its present position between Montpellier Street and Bays Hill Road, and its success was largely due to Miss Dorothea Beale. For almost fifty years, from 1858, she ruled over its growth and development, and her work had a very considerable effect on female education in England as a whole.

▲ Cheltenham, The College Playing Fields 1907 59038

A sizeable crowd are fully engrossed in the action of a cricket match on the playing fields of the College, against the backdrop of the buildings, all of which are contained on an 85-acre site. The College was founded in 1841. The crowded stand, erected in front of the yellow brick gymnasium with its two towers, indicates that this is probably a match between county teams held during the annual Cheltenham Cricket Festival, rather than one between College sides.

◄ **Cheltenham, London Road 1906** 54321
A number 14 double-decker electric tram trundles along the leafy London Road, whose tree-lined pavements underline the reason why Cheltenham has justifiably earned the sobriquet the Garden Town. The terraces here had all been constructed by 1820.

Cheltenham, High Street 1901 47265

Up until 1779, Cheltenham was only a small market town with this single High Street lined with brick houses and shops. Not until George III's visit in 1788 did the town become fashionable and the process of speculative building investment begin.

Cheltenham, High Street 1901 47266

Even at the beginning of the 19th century, the little River Chelt still flowed down the centre of this street, causing considerable inconvenience to shop owners and customers alike.

Cheltenham, High Street 1906 54319
These three photographs, taken a century later, show how much of the elegance and architectural splendours of the adjacent areas north and south failed to penetrate this commercial centre. By 1906 the central roadway had been paved, and electric trams were operating along this stretch of the London to Tewkesbury road.

Eastern Gloucestershire

**Chipping Campden
High Street c1950** C335035
This typical Cotswold town, with its buildings of pale grey and
cream limestone, was one of the great wool towns of the Middle
Ages before becoming a thriving market centre. The name
'Chipping' means market. The Noel Arms, on the extreme right and
on the south side of the street, is of 18th-century construction,
and has a lamp suspended above the original carriage entrance.

Moreton-in-Marsh, Curfew Tower c1960 M244192
The stone Curfew Tower, on the right and on the corner of Oxford Street, is 16th-century and probably the oldest building in the town. In its gabled turret is a clock dated 1648 and a bell dated 1633, which was rung daily up until 1860.

Moreton-in-Marsh, High Street c1950 M244038
The broad High Street is part of the Fosse Way, and is dominated by the Redesdale Market Hall, a fine Victorian Tudor building designed by Sir Ernest George in 1887. To the left, with twin flagpoles at each end of its frontage is the Redesdale Arms Hotel, built in the late 18th century and one of the principal coaching inns of the time.

◀ **Lower Slaughter
The Mill c1955** L313010
In the foreground is one
of the weathered stone
bridges which cross the
brook at intervals as it
flows through the village.
Beyond is the tall brick
chimney of the early
19th-century mill,
powered by a
waterwheel.

◀ **Lower Slaughter, The Green c1955** L313007
The Slaughter brook runs down the middle of this village - one of the loveliest in the county, despite its ugly name. It is allegedly derived either from the name of the Lord of the Manor in the 12th century, 'de Sclotre', or from the quantities of sloe-trees which were a feature of the surrounding landscape.

▼ **Bourton-on-the-Water, The Village 1948**
B392035
Just off the Fosse Way, this village, once the site of a Roman settlement, clusters around the banks of the wide, shallow Windrush, which is crossed by a number of simple footbridges, some of which are only two hundred and fifty years old.

◀ **Northleach, Market Square c1955** N125013
Northleach was once one of the most prosperous wool towns of the Cotswolds in the 15th century, and an important cross-roads of the Fosse Way and the London-Cheltenham roads. It suffered traffic problems until the recent construction of its bypass. The Market Square was probably the site of the quarry for the stone from which its magnificent church of St Peter and St Paul was built.

Bibury, Arlington Mill c1955 B530025

Now a folk museum and art gallery, the mill was probably built in the early 17th century on a Domesday site. It is recorded in 1638 as a fulling mill for cloth, before being used for corn. The projecting cottage was added around 1700, and the roof was altered in the 19th century, when the stone buttresses were added along with additional support from iron columns and girders.

Chedworth, St Andrew's Church c1960 C446015

This is a late Norman church, which was subsequently augmented during the 14th and 15th centuries by the wealth generated by the local wool trade. The three lower stages of the bell tower are Norman; the upper stage is 13th-century and the parapet is 15th-century. The most outstanding feature is the fine Perpendicular windows on the south side, which were reputedly installed by the Neville family in 1490.

Chedworth, Church Row c1960 C466014
This fine row of mid 18th-century Cotswold stone cottages is situated in the lane leading to the church of St Andrew; the roof of the nearest building is evidently in urgent need of repair.

Colesbourne, Lower Hilcot c1960 C453012
Three mallard ducks purposefully traverse the shallow ford across this little stream which flows on to join the River Thames. The wooden posts are positioned to assist coaches at times when these waters are in flood, although the abandoned cartwheel suggests that not all vehicles made the crossing successfully.

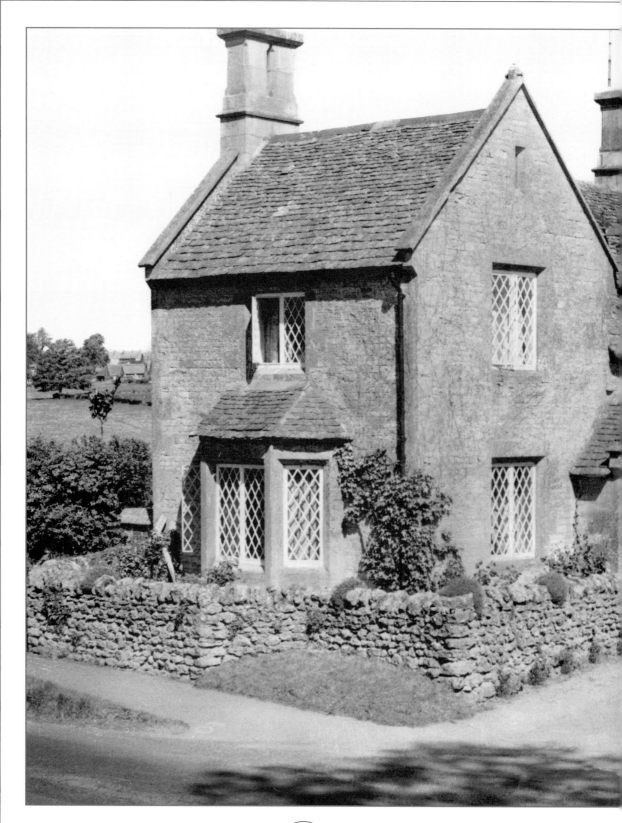

**Colesbourne
The Post Office c1960**

C453005
The cream-painted standard telephone box provides an incongruous contrast to its setting outside this small Post Office; it is attached to the Victorian lodge on the outskirts of the Colesbourne estate, where Henry J Elwes planted his famous arboretum.

Cirencester and its Environs

Cirencester, Market Place 1898 40965

Cirencester
The Royal Agricultural College 1898 40988
A mile outside Cirencester, on the Bath road, these two imposing Tudor-style blocks with their central tower were opened in 1846. Over succeeding decades, they were to take a leading role in the advancement of scientific agriculture. A third block, the George V wing, was added in 1936.

◀ **Cirencester Park, Earl of Bathurst's Hounds 1898** 40987
An alert pack of foxhounds of the local Vale of the White Horse Hunt are being exercised by their three handlers in readiness for the approaching hunting season. On the extreme left of this remarkably static group of dogs is a Jack Russell terrier, used for extracting foxes from their earths after they have gone to ground.

◄ Cirencester Park, Oxen Team 1898 40986
Although working bullocks were used on Cotswold farms well into the last century, particularly for compressing streambeds and millponds, those used on Lord Bathurst's estate for ploughing were regarded as a something of an anachronism, even though these huge beasts consumed less than horses and possessed greater stamina.

▼ Cirencester, Castle Street 1899 44834
The late 19th-century Post Office dominates this photograph of Castle Street in brilliant sunshine. On the opposite side of the street, an assortment of hardware and farm equipment is displayed in the doorway of a shop. Further along, a barber's striped pole projects over the pavement.

◄ Cirencester, Market Place 1898 40965
The richly embellished 15th-century tower of St John the Baptist, soaring to 132 feet, rises above the Market Place; the church's ornate south porch is flanked by Georgian facades. On the extreme right, the Fleece Hotel comprises two buildings of differing styles. One is early 17th-century, with a stucco front painted in imitation half-timbering, and the other is 18th-century.

Cirencester
Castle Street 1898 40971
The photographer's work attracts attention from bystanders outside Jeffries' emporium, while carts make their way with difficulty over the roadway which is being resurfaced. Lloyd's Bank can be seen on the bend of the street behind. A fine example of Palladian architecture, it was originally a wool-merchant's house before being transformed into Pitt, Bowly and Croome's bank in around 1790.

Cirencester
Gloucester Street 1898 42362
A heavily-laden cart makes its way along Gloucester Street,
past the almshouses and quaint cottages with their Cotswold
stone slates. These were once occupied by the drowners,
men who looked after the water meadows.

Duntisbourne Abbots
The Church c1960 D161010
St Peter's Church was once a possession of Gloucester Abbey,
and its tower and parts of the interior are Norman; its 13th-century
chancel has been extensively rebuilt. The church was heavily
restored in 1872. In spite of its small size, the fact that it is built on
a slope towards the River Dun has allowed for the construction of a
crypt beneath the chancel.

Duntisbourne Abbots, The Village c1960 D161009
Many of the houses and cottages in this lovely village are of considerable age, with the manor house and several other buildings dating from the 17th century. The neatly-clipped yews stand at the entrance to the churchyard.

Bisley, The Church 1910 62694
Dating mainly from the 13th and 14th centuries, and with a lofty spire dating from the time of Agincourt, the church of All Saints was extensively restored in 1862 by the Reverend W H Lowder, who had been Thomas Keble's curate in 1860-64. It was the latter who instituted the custom of holding daily services; this custom was later adopted by John Henry Newman at Oxford.

Bisley, The Old Bone House 1910 62695
This hexagonal stone structure in the churchyard of All Saints dates from the 13th century, and is more accurately described as a Poor Soul's Light. Candles were installed in the openings to enable masses to be said for the poor. It is thought to be the only one in England surviving out of doors. It is built over a vault where disinterred bones were dumped when old graves were broken open. Legend has it that the local priest fell into it one night and died. As a result, the then Pope decreed that there should be no more burials at Bisley for two years, and villagers were obliged to journey fifteen miles to Bibury to place their dead in 'Bisley piece'.

Bisley, The Wells 1910 62696
This structure bears the inscription 'Bless ye the Lord, praise Him and magnify'; these seven springs emerge via five recesses and two spouts. They were still clearly in use by villagers in the early part of the 20th century for the provision of drinking water. On Ascension Day each year, a blessing ceremony takes place at the well.

Bisley, High Street 1910 62697
The steep High Street, running north to south, is lined with closely-built houses, mainly of the 17th century. Bisley was once a Royal manor, and an important centre for the local woollen industry.

◄ **Chalford, The Church
1890** 25169
The newly re-roofed
Romanesque church
with its curiously short
broach-spire is viewed
from the towpath of the
canal, which makes its
way towards Stroud.

◄ **Chalford, The Church 1900** 45588
Built in 1724, Christ Church, on the left, with its broach spire, was extensively modified in 1841 and 1857 before being re-roofed and again altered ten years before this photograph was taken. The circular building on the right used to be the house of a canal lengthsman, or maintenance man.

▼ **Chalford, The Golden Valley 1910** 62709
The Frome Valley, dotted with mills and with the Thames and Severn Canal running through it, has long been a centre of industry. Chalford itself stands on the steep north bank. Many of the wealthy clothiers' 19th-century houses were built on terraces cut into the hillside, with the result that the front doors are several storeys above the garden entrances.

◄ **Chalford On the Canal 1910** 62711
Several small boys and girls are sitting beside the canal. In the past it was once busy with an incessant stream of barges passing through this now-abandoned lock, laden with bales of cloth. Along the crest of the hill are the homes of the mill owners, while the workers and the mills themselves were positioned in the valley bottom.

Chalford
On the Canal 1910 62712
The two pubs, the Bell Inn and the New Red Lion Inn, would have serviced
the needs of the mill workers at the end of their long working day.

Chalford, The Village 1910 62713
Two patient donkeys, which were used for transporting essential household supplies such as bread, milk and coal up the steep and narrow streets of Chalford, are posed for the photographer by their driver against the backdrop of the wooded slopes on the far side of the valley. The autumnal tints of the trees inspired the descriptive title of the Golden Valley.

▼ **Chalford, The Golden Valley 1890** 25166
In this panoramic view of the Golden Valley, the mill chimneys are
visible in the background; the workers' cottages are on the lower
slopes of the hill, and the canal winds its way along the valley bottom.

▼ **Minchinhampton, Market House 1901** 47348
Market House was built in 1698 to house the local wool market by Philip Sheppard,
whose ancestor Samuel had bought the manor of Minchinhampton in 1651. It is
supported on stone pillars with a row of wooden columns in the centre, and is
surrounded by a collection of 17th- and 18th-century hotels and town houses. The
actress Sarah Siddons reputedly performed in the room above, which is now,
appropriately, the home of the local amateur dramatic society.

▲ **Minchinhampton, Holy
Trinity Church 1901**
47350
The church was given by
William the Conqueror to
the Abbaye aux Dames in
Caen, who administered it
until 1415; it was then in
the care of the nuns of
Syon Abbey until the
Dissolution. The curious
14th-century octagonal
spire was reduced by fifty
feet to its present height
in 1543, when it was in
danger of collapsing, and
was then capped with its
coronet.

**Brimscombe
The Valley 1900** 45590
Along with the hamlets of
Burleigh, Hyde, Cowcombe
and Wall's Quarry,
Brimscombe was formed
into a separate parish out of
Minchinhampton and
Rodborough in 1840. The
19th-century mill buildings
in the bottom of the valley
are set along a stretch of
the Thames and Severn
canal; this was once an
important inland port.

**Brimscombe
Wall's Quarry 1901**
47364
The stone houses of
this small hamlet are
spread along the steep
hillside, with the
Romanesque tower of
Holy Trinity church
visible above the trees
in the middle
foreground.

Gloucester and its Environs

Birdlip, The Village 1907 59061
This little hamlet, six miles south-east of Gloucester, stands on the Ermine Way, and appears to have been a posting station during the Roman occupation. It was certainly on a major coaching route in subsequent centuries, and only the construction of the bypass, which opened in 1988, has relieved it of the heavy traffic which used to thunder along this main street.

Birdlip, The George Hotel 1907 59062
At the western end of the village, the 19th-century Royal George Hotel stands close to the edge of the steep escarpment of the Cotswolds, where the 17th-century coach road plunges down a 1 in 5 slope towards Gloucester; it was therefore an important stopping place for horse-drawn traffic.

Cranham, Cranham Woods 1907 59066
The spectacular beauty of the beech woods near the village of Cranham, particularly in autumn when the foliage changes colour, has long attracted visitors. The composer Gustav Holst used to come here from Cheltenham to walk; he dedicated his setting of Christina Rossetti's carol 'In the Bleak Midwinter' to Cranham.

Hucclecote, The Village c1965 H337004
Originally the site of a Roman villa in the 1st or 2nd century AD, and on Ermine Street, this outlying hamlet has gradually been absorbed into expanding Gloucester; many of its older houses have been demolished to make way for modern development. But as the sign on the left indicates, the old craft of handloom weaving is still practised here.

▼ **Gloucester, The Cathedral 1892** 29899
The splendid Norman tower of the Cathedral rises above the roofs of the
county town, forming an important part of the city's skyline. The
foundation stone of the building was laid in 1089, and the great structure
has been augmented and restored over the succeeding centuries.

▼ **Gloucester, Westgate Street 1891** 29004
Only the distinctive three-stage Perpendicular tower of St Nicholas Church, in the
centre of the picture, serves as a major landmark in this street - it has been
radically changed during the past half-century by piecemeal development. More
than twenty-five listed buildings of historical or architectural interest have been
demolished since the end of the Second World War.

▲ **Gloucester, Southgate
Street 1904** 51987
An electric tram, bound
for the Circus, passes the
three-gabled, half-
timbered and overhanging
frontage of the 16th-
century house where
Robert Raikes, the founder
of the Sunday School
Movement, lived between
1768 and 1801. On the
left, close to the offices of
the Liverpool and London
Insurance Offices, an
unsaddled horse takes a
close interest in a
conversation between its
handler and a smartly-
dressed matron.

◀ **Gloucester**
Northgate Street 1904
51988
18th- and 19th-century
shops and offices, along
with a plethora of
advertising signs, provide
the backdrop to this busy
street scene at the
beginning of the Edwardian
era. Since in 1910 there
were still only ten thousand
motor vehicles registered in
Great Britain, horse-drawn
transport still held sway.

**Gloucester
Eastgate Street 1931**
83828
St Michael's Tower rises
above the shops of
Eastgate Street. The
motor vehicle is for the
first time predominant
in this early thirties
photograph, giving a
clear indication of its
growing importance.
Nevertheless, the two
delivery boys on their
bicycles outside the
Saracen's Head Hotel
show that commercial
traffic has yet to
supplant pedal power.

Gloucester, The Docks 1912 65114
Queen Elizabeth I gave Gloucester the formal status of a port in 1580, but it was not until the completed construction of the Gloucester and Berkeley Canal in 1827 that the city began to equal Bristol in importance as a grain port.

Gloucester, The Docks 1923 73689
The three commodious docks, the largest of which was opened in 1892, remained busy until the eventual decline in trade. The area has been preserved and restored, and is now a major heritage attraction for tourists.

Gloucester
Raikes's Sunday School 1923 73687
This half-timbered cottage in St Catherine's Street is where Robert Raikes first held his Sunday school, which these young children may have attended. Widely, if questionably, regarded as the founder of the Sunday School Movement, he is buried in the church of St. Mary de Crypt.

Stroud
and the
Vale
of Berkeley

Berkeley, Market Place 1904 51750
The wide, straight street of Berkeley is lined with houses of the Georgian period or earlier, with the 19th-century Town Hall facing out onto the Market Place. An assortment of four farm wagons, one with a load of hay, serve to underline the fact that horse-drawn transport prevailed in this Edwardian era.

◄ **Ham**
Old Cottages 1904
51755
This small parish in the Berkeley Vale consists of isolated farms and cottages, including these quaint brick two-storey buildings with their thatched roofs and inclined dormer windows. They were probably built in the 17th or early 18th centuries, and were occupied by local farm workers.

Berkeley, The Castle c1955 B72033

This was originally an 11th-century Anglo-Saxon manor belonging to Earl Godwin; after the Norman Conquest, it was entrusted to William FitzOsbern as part of the western defences against the Welsh. He formed the foundations of the present keep, which dates from 1153, but Thomas, 8th Lord Berkeley, remodelled the whole of the interior between 1340-1350. He was Lord here when Edward II was imprisoned, tortured and horribly murdered in a cell off the state apartments and Great Hall in 1327.

Frampton on Severn, Thatched Cottages c1955 F142204

The wide, long, flat village green extends over twenty-two acres. It is bordered by picturesque half-timbered, thatched cottages like these, making this one of the most attractive villages in South Gloucestershire. The beautiful Rosamund de Clifford, the 'Fair Rosamund' and mistress of Henry II, was born and raised here. According to legend she was forced to take poison by Henry's wife Eleanor, and died in 1177 at Woodstock.

Frampton on Severn Frampton Court c1955

F142208

This Palladian mansion occupies the site of the ancient family mansion of the Cliffords. It was built between 1731-33 for Richard Clutterbuck, an official of the Bristol Customs House, probably by the architect John Strahan, who was inspired by Vanbrugh. The grounds contain a statue of Fair Rosamund by a lily pond, and local legend tells of a secret passage running from here to the 15th-century manor house on the green.

▼ Frampton on Severn, The Manor Farm c1955 F142212

On the north side of the green, this mid 15th-century manor farmhouse was the home of the Clifford family. The ground floor of the main building is of stone with mullioned windows; above it the timber-framed upper storeys project with close-set studding. The adjoining barn is probably also from the same period.

▼ Stroud, Bowbridge 1890 25152

In the foreground is Bowbridge, the southern suburb of Stroud, with the chimneys of several small textile mills clearly visible; the main town is prominent on the hillside beyond. Throughout the 18th and 19th centuries, Stroud was the capital of the Cotswold cloth industry: at its zenith it had more than a hundred and fifty mills in operation.

▲ Stroud, High Street 1910 62676

The steep, winding and narrow High Street (down which flaming tar barrels were rolled to the terror of the populace until the practice was banned in 1824) gives an excellent impression of the variety of trades which were offered in the Edwardian era. On the extreme left is a baker's and corn and flour merchant, while next door at No 21 is a brush, rope and twine merchant. On the corner, Hillier's the butcher advertises its bacon curing operation. On the right, Smith's the chemist is next door to the double-fronted grocery, wine and spirit merchants.

◀ **Stroud, High Street c1950** S224023

A policeman stands on point duty at the junction of Lansdown, King Street, the High Street, and Gloucester Street, with the Greyhound Inn, built by the Stroud brewery in 1904, on the extreme left of the picture. Diagonally opposite, the Victorian frontage of part of A E Gardner's store has been transferred to Baker's shoeshop. Further up the High Street are local branches of Hepworth's tailoring and Timothy White's the chemists.

Stroud, King Street 1910 62677
We are looking along King Street from the same junction. The High Street is to the left, and the extensive premises of Gardner's general store, with its hanging lamps suspended over the pavement, leads on to the premises of Dale Forty's music shop. On the opposite side of the road is the then recently-opened Green Dragon inn, with its signboard hanging from an ornate wrought iron fixture.

Stroud, High Street c1950 S224010
Here we have another view of the steep and narrow High Street. On the left are the open-fronted premises and marble slabs of the local branch of Mac Fisheries, a national chain of fishmongers. Two doors further along is Hepworths, the clothing outfitters, and at the bend is a branch of Timothy Whites, the chemists.

◄ Stroud, King Street 1925 77562

Outside the extensive premises of Lewis & Godrey's clothing store, a No 51 charabanc and its white-coated and booted driver prepares to take on passengers. Just beyond is the cupola above the premises of Lloyd's bank. Above the store, a board advertises the Admiralty serges for which the local textile industry is famous.

▼ Stroud Sim's Clock c1950 S224013

The clock was a bequest to the town by William Thomas Sim, a retired local grocer, civic leader and philanthropist, who died in 1917 at the age of seventy-nine. The twenty-four foot-high monument was built of Bath stone by the firm of H H Martin of Cheltenham, and was completed in 1921. It stands at the junction of five roads. Mr Sim's will also provided for the annual sum of £5 to be paid to a firm of local jewellers for the winding of the clock.

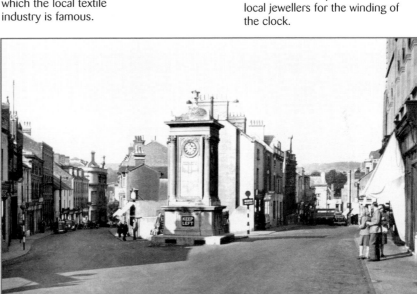

◄ Stroud George Street 1910 62678

A farm trap and a carriage with a liveried coachman make their way along George Street past the imposing façade of the Wilts and Dorset Bank, on the left, and the Brooklyn Cycle Depot across the unsurfaced road. A uniformed sailor window-shops below the blind of the emporium on the corner of Bedford Street.

◄ **Painswick
The Village c1950**

P3045

Four miles north of Stroud, and ten miles south of Gloucester, Painswick was a centre for the cloth industry; it developed into a small town during the 17th century. Along with the spacious homes of the wealthy clothiers, there are small streets like this one comprising small shops and homely dwellings.

Rodborough
The Village c1950 R3110007

A mile south of Stroud, and at the top of the steep hill leading up from Bowbridge, we see this fine group of stone cottages. The Prince Albert Hotel, named after the Prince Consort, sells beers brewed by the local Stroud Brewery. Two of the mullioned windows on the ground floor had already been altered to allow for the introduction of ventilation fans.

Slad, The Valley 1910
62708

This picturesque hillside village was to be immortalised in English literature in 'Cider with Rosie', the first novel of Laurie Lee, who was born here four years after this picture was taken. An account of his childhood years, his book charts the changes in this rural settlement during the 1920s, including the death of the last squire, who lived at the 18th-century house called Steanbridge.

Bussage
The Church 1910
62699

The 19th-century church of St Michael stands on a steep hill, and was built of snicked stone. The monies for its construction were largely raised from subscriptions by Oxford undergraduates, at the request of Thomas Keble. The porch and the three-bay south aisle were added in 1854 by G F Bodley.

◄ **Amberley**
The Village 1901 47357
This village of scattered houses on a steep hillside some seven hundred feet above sea level has two noted literary associations. P C Wren, the author of 'Beau Geste', is buried in Holy Trinity's churchyard, and the 18th-century Rose Cottage was the home of the Victorian novelist Dinah Mulock (Mrs Craik) while she wrote her opus 'John Halifax, Gentleman'. Much of the action was set here and at nearby Amberley Court.

◄ **Amberley**
The Castle 1899 42554
This castle, probably dating from the 13th century, stands on the high ridge overlooking the Woodchester Valley, just north of Nailsworth and on the western edge of Minchinhampton Common. It is now privately owned.

▼ **Woodchester**
The Village 1890 25173
This is a typical wool village of the region. On the extreme right we can see the chimney of one of the 18th- and 19th-century textile mills which were situated in the valley bottom beside the River Frome; the weavers' cottages occupied the hillside above. The village was also the site of two monasteries: one for Dominican and the other for Franciscan monks.

◄ **Woodchester**
The Church 1890 25174
The church of St Mary was built in 1863; it replaced a nearby Norman building constructed on the site of a sumptuous sixty-room Roman villa, which was excavated in the late 18th century. Beneath the old churchyard is the famous Orpheus pavement; a polychrome mosaic showing Orpheus playing a lyre; it is made up of one and a half million half-inch cubes. It is periodically uncovered by a local group for public display.

◄ **Tetbury, Church Street c1949** T155027
Close to the Wiltshire border, this little market and wool town has retained many of its 17th- and 18th-century buildings, such as the Eight Bells Inn, seen here on the right. Its plastered façade probably conceals timber-framed construction beneath, and is jettied out over a pillared arcade.

◀ **Nailsworth**
Bridge Street c1950 N1004
Built at the junction of two valleys, Nailsworth represents the transition between the old wool-based industry and more modern industries. As a consequence, most of the buildings here are less then two hundred years old. On the right, Davis the jeweller's and watchmaker's displays its wares, while on the opposite side of the street are advertising hoardings promoting a football match between Swindon and Port Vale and the Bath Horse Show.

▼ **Uley, From Uley Bury**
1900 45539
Here we have a panoramic view of this lovely village, whose handloom weavers produced some of England's finest broadcloth in the 18th century. Viewed from the 23-acre Iron Age fort which stands on the steep road leading north-west away from the village, the church of St Giles stands out to the left of the picture.

◀ **Uley, The Green and the Church 1904** 51953
This view looks down the hill into the village. The Old Crown Inn and the adjoining cottages are faced by the Georgian houses on the other side of the green. The church of St Giles, with its north tower and unusual octagonal spirelet, was rebuilt between 1857-8 by S S Teulon, and overlooks the Uley valley.

Dursley, The Town 1900 45519
One of the former main centres of textile production between the 15th and 18th centuries, Dursley was also briefly a butter market. It was saved from economic decline by the arrival of the engineering firm of R A Lister at the beginning of the last century. The tower of St James's church, rebuilt in 1707, rises above the shops, houses and mills of the town.

Dursley, Long Street c1950 D72031
This view looks down the hill towards The Priory and Lister's factory. The 18th-century shopfronts of Long Street have been largely retained. The three-storied brick Old Bell Hotel, on the left, sports two Venetian-style windows on its ground floor, while those above have rounded heads.

Dursley, Parsonage Street c1950 D72035
The roughcast Market House and Town Hall of 1738, with its open arcade, bell-turret and cupola, is overshadowed by the 18th-century tower of St James's church. The original spire and medieval tower collapsed in January 1689; the tower was rebuilt by Thomas Sumsion of Colerne between 1707-9, including the openwork battlements and pinnacles in the style of the Gloucester Coronet.

**Wotton-under-Edge
Church Street 1897**

39385

The sharp escarpment of the Cotswolds looms above the town. It was known locally as 'Woulton-under-Ridge' in the reign of Henry III, when it first began to prosper as a market and trade centre. Outside the newsagent's and tobacconist's shop on the left, a placard for the regional newspaper advertises a report on the parliamentary progress of the Boundaries Bill.

▼ **Wotton-under-Edge, Church Street 1900** 46308
As in picture No 39385, the photographer's activities grip the attention of all those present - with the exception of a border collie, who only has eyes for his master standing beside the laden cart. On the far side of the street are the almshouses bequeathed to the town by the former Sheriff of London Hugh Perry, who held the office in 1632. They were intended to house six poor men and six poor women of the town. A central domed cupola surmounts their six gables, each with its finial. Beyond is the Jolly Reaper inn.

▼ **Wotton-under-Edge, Long Street 1897** 39384
Boxes of Fry's cocoa are piled in the doorway of W Rogers' Golden Tea Warehouse on the right, and an assortment of children and adults have paused in the early afternoon to watch the photographer at work. At the top of the street stands an elegant 18th-century building housing the police station; on the near left, an outfitter's shop displays lengths of cloth. The cobble-lined open gutters are partially paved to enable customers to reach the shops without unnecessary and ungainly exertion.

▲ **Wotton-under-Edge Long Street 1903** 49796
Six years after picture No 39384 was taken, the most notable change to the view lies in the resurfacing and repair of the pavements and guttering on both sides of the street. The distinctive cupola and copper dragon weathervane of 1859 rises above the Tolsey House on the corner of Market Street. This 17th-century house was used for the market court and as a lock-up. Facing it is the White Lion Hotel.

◄ **Wotton-under-Edge,
Long Street 1897** 39382
This continuation of the High
Street shows some of the
18th-century facades and
shopfronts that were applied
to the original Tudor houses.
Outside Fowles the draper's
shop, a two-wheeled milk
cart prepares to tackle the
steep slope ahead.

Wotton-under-Edge Long Street 1903

49798

An open topped carter's wagon and its load of passengers makes its way down Long Street in the early afternoon, according to the large clock on Tolsey House in the background. It is about to pass the twin-gabled 17th-century Berkeley House at 31 Long Street. Although it has no connection with the local Berkeley family, a speculator bought it in 1922, and its contents were removed. The Victoria and Albert Museum in London purchased one of the rooms -it has green-painted pine panelling and 18th-century Chinese wallpaper. Another oak-panelled room was bought by an American museum.

◀ **Wotton-under-Edge Kingswood Abbey 1897**
39391
This 15th-century gatehouse is in the village of Kingswood, one mile south of Wotton; it is part of the Cistercian abbey which existed here until the Dissolution. It has shallow pinnacled buttresses and a skilfully-carved canopy above the mullioned window, whose central motif is carved in the shape of a branching lily; the symbol of the Virgin to whom the abbey was dedicated. It is now used as a council chamber.

◄ **Wotton-under-Edge Market Street 1897** 39381
This revealing glimpse looks down Market Street towards the High Street. The Town Hall, built in 1872, is on the right, with an advertising placard promoting an Agricultural Show at Berkeley Castle attached to its frontage. The right to hold a market and fair was granted to Maurice, Lord Berkeley by Henry III, and was responsible for the subsequent prosperity of the town.

▼ **Wotton-under-Edge Tortworth Court 1897** 39393
The Victorian Gothic mansion of Tortworth Court, with its distinctive welcoming gatehouse, was built in the mid 19th century following the elevation to the peerage of the first Earl of Dulcie in 1837, and became the family seat. It was taken over by the Admiralty during the Second World War, and part of the surrounding estate was subsequently transformed into Layhill Prison. The mansion is now being developed as a luxury hotel.

◄ **North Nibley, The Tyndale Monument 1897** 39390
Two carefully-posed groups of young girls are a feature of this photograph of the village of North Nibley, with the 111 foot-high memorial tower to the martyr William Tyndale on the knoll behind. Erected in 1866, it commemorates his life's work in translating the Bible into English; an endeavour for which he eventually died in 1536 at Vilvorde in Flanders, where he was strangled and burnt at the stake for heresy.

Alderley
The Village 1904
53139
This village, whose
cottages have their
windows wide open to
the autumn sunshine,
was for long the home
of the Hale family,
including Sir Matthew
Hale, the 'Upright Judge'
of the turbulent 17th
century.

Alderley, The Village 1904 53138
This picturesque mill hamlet was also the residence of the noted botanist and painter Marianne North. A contemporary of the naturalist Charles Darwin, she travelled the world extensively and was buried in the local churchyard in 1890.

The Severn Valley and the Vale of Leadon

Dymock
The Village c1955 D162006
This small village is close to the Herefordshire boundary, on the banks of the River Leadon, and in the heart of Gloucestershire's daffodil crescent. The early Norman church of St Mary can be seen in the background. Dymock boasts one of the oldest inhabited buildings in Gloucestershire, the 15th-century cruck cottage in the middle left of the picture. The village is also famous for the discovery of an occult 17th-century curse. Scratched on a piece of thin lead, it was found concealed near a chimney in Wilton Place in 1892. The curse is directed at one Sarah Ellis; local legend has it that she is buried at a nearby crossroads with a stake through her heart.

Newent
The Market House c1950 N180012
This late Tudor market house, at the centre of this bustling town,
was restored in the middle of the 19th century. Supported on
sixteen wooden pillars, its single, large upstairs room is reached by
a flight of outside stairs.

Newent, Church Street c1955 N180034
The black-and-white market hall is clearly visible at the end of the street. The 18th-century brick frontage of the George Hotel stands on the left, with the entrance to its cobbled stable yard just beyond. On the right, the hanging sign of H Bray's general hardware store is adjacent to the small garage; at the start of the 20th century, the garage was a butcher's shop and slaughterhouse.

Newent, Broad Street c1965 N180064
On the right, the imposing 18th-century brick frontage of Lloyd's Bank, with its stone pediment and columned entrance, faces the small shops across the road. Near the dogleg bend in the road is the local branch of the International Stores grocery chain, and also the Red Lion pub with its hanging sign.

Huntley, Huntley Manor c1955 H338002
Built in 1862 by S S Teulon for the Ackers family, this substantial mansion resembles a French chateau, with its turrets and ornamental iron finials. The original owner, who was a keen aboriculturist, planted the surrounding grounds with a wide variety of trees and shrubs. His son, C P Ackers, shared his enthusiasm; he went on to found a local wood-working business and nursery and to write one of the standard books on forestry. The house underwent sympathetic restoration nine years after this photograph was taken.

Huntley, The Church and the School c1955

H338013

Shaded by tall conifers, only the tower of the 12th-century church of St John the Baptist still stands. The remainder of the building was demolished in 1861; it was rebuilt by S S Teulon using the old red sandstone of the district, and Painswick stone for the spire. The adjacent school building was constructed in 1875.

◄ **Cinderford
High Street c1965**
C448025
Cinderford is one of the
two main towns in the
Forest of Dean; its name
reflects its involvement
in the coal mining and
iron working industries
of the area, whose
history reaches back to
before Roman times.

Mitcheldean, The Village c1955 M246013

The 18th-century spire of the 15th-century St Michael's Church soars above this small former market town on the north-east border of the Forest of Dean, where it nestles snugly into the surrounding hills. On those to the west, at Whigpool Common, an unsuccessful attempt to mine gold was made prior to the First World War.

West Dean, Speech House c1955 F146020

Overlooking the Cannop Valley, this building was originally a lodge housing the Court of Speech for the Forest of Dean, and was first used in 1680 for a session of the Mine Law Court. By 1858, it had expanded into an inn catering for those attending the court; it was extended and enlarged in the latter part of the 19th century. The monument in the foreground commemorates the planting of an oak tree by the Prince Consort in 1861.

Newnham, Flaxley Abbey c1955 N87007

Incorporating fragments of a 12th-century Cistercian abbey, this battlemented and ivy-clad house with its partial moat is roughly L-shaped. The abbey was founded by the second son of the Earl of Hereford in memory of his father, who was killed on this spot while hunting on Christmas Eve in 1145. After the Dissolution, the abbey was owned and remodelled by the Boevey family, and the southern wing was added in the late 18th century.

Lydney, The Berkeley Viaduct c1955 L200024
The last railway bridge to cross the River Severn before the open sea, it linked Sharpness and Lydney. It was built as part of the old Great Western Railway between 1875-9, and consisted of two main spans of 327 feet and nineteen lesser spans, with a steam-operated swinging section over the Gloucester to Berkeley Canal. An oil barge struck it in 1960, and two of the spans were brought down. The remainder was subsequently demolished.

◀ **Lydney, Hill Street c1950** L200006
The main street of Lydney, with its dark sandstone and slate-roofed buildings, presents a rather dour aspect. The Railway Inn, on the left, offering bed and breakfast accommodation and luncheons; it demonstrates its earlier links with Lydney Junction Station on the Severn & Wye Railway, the only one in the district.

Lydney, The Cross and the Town Hall c1955

L200029

The 14th-century cross, on its original base and at the top of eight stone steps, underwent restoration in 1878. The Town Hall, across the road, dates from 1888; it mirrors the ogee arch of the cross in its own flat-fronted entrance. It was a gift to the town from the Bathurst family.

▼ Lydney, Newerne Street c1950 L200018

◀ Brockweir, The Village c1955 B533016

The little hamlet of Brockweir, straggling along the floor of the Wye Valley and with a utilitarian bridge spanning the river itself, lies on the county border with Gwent. The three-storey gabled Manor House dates from the 16th century and faces onto the bridge.

Beachley, The Severn Bridge c1965 B38005
Opened in 1966, and designed by Sir Gilbert Roberts, this innovative structure is capable of carrying vehicles of up to two hundred tons in weight. It has a main span of 3,240 feet and two side spans of 1,000 feet. The two towers are both 400 feet high. Although roughly the same size and capacity as the Forth Road Bridge of 1964, it weighs about a third less, and was considerably cheaper to construct.

Beachley, The Ferry c1955   B38330

Prior to the building of the Severn Bridge, which now sweeps above the peninsula of Beachley Point, this little powered ferry carried small vehicles across the Severn to the outskirts of Aust on the eastern bank.

Beachley, The Slipway c1955   B38331

Blakeney, High Street c1955 B523004
At the time of the Norman Conquest, Blakeney was one of the tithings of the low-lying parish of Awre, but it is now a separate ecclesiastical entity. The main A48, linking Gloucester and Chepstow, runs through the town; these dangerous bends were often the scene of serious accidents, until road improvements were made.

Blakeney
High Street and the Church c1955 B523033
The church of All Saints was originally built in the early 18th
century, but was remodelled by Samuel Hewlett in around 1820,
and further restored in 1907. Its small tower is out of proportion to
the remainder of the building.

Coleford
The Church Tower and the Memorial c1950 C315034
The gardens enclosing the war memorial delineate the shape of the
former octagonal parish church which stood here. Built in 1821 by
Richard James, it was demolished sixty-one years later, except for
its tower with its clock and embattled parapet with pinnacles.

Coleford
The Town Hall c1950 C315027
An open-topped three-wheeled car heads towards the 17th-century
Town Hall, which was rebuilt in 1866 on its island site. The tower of
the former parish church is visible beyond.

Index

Alderley 92-93, 94-95

Amberley 78-79

Beachley 108, 109

Berkeley 66-67, 68-69

Bibury 34

Birdlip 56-57, 58

Bisley 45, 46, 47

Blakeney 110-111, 112

Bourton-on-the-Water 33

Brimscombe 53, 54-55

Brockweir 107

Bussage 77

Chalford 48-49, 50, 51, 52

Chedworth 34, 35

Cheltenham 22, 23, 24, 25, 26-27, 28, 29

Chipping Campden 30

Cinderford 102

Cirencester 38-39, 40-41, 42, 43

Cirencester Park 40-41

Cleeve Hill 19

Coleford 113, 114

Colesbourne 35, 36-37

Cranham 59

Deerhurst 14-15

Duntisbourne Abbots 44, 45

Dursley 82, 83

Dymock 96

Frampton 69, 70

Gloucester 60-61, 62-63, 64, 65

Ham 68

Hucclecote 59

Huntley 99, 100-101

Leckhampton 21

Lower Slaughter 32-33

Lydney 104-105, 106-107

Minchinhampton 52-53

Mitcheldean 102-103

Moreton-in-Marsh 31

Nailsworth 80-81

Newent 97, 98

Newnham 103

Northleach 33

North Nibley 91

Painswick 76

Prestbury 20-21

Rodborough 76-77

Slad 77

Southam 19

Stroud 70-71, 72-73, 74-75

Tetbury 80

Tewkesbury 16-17, 18-19

Uley 81

West Dean 103

Winchcombe 18

Woodchester 79

Wooton-under-edge 84-85, 86-87, 88-89, 90-91

Frith Book Co Titles

www.frithbook.co.uk

The Frith Book Company publishes over 100 new titles each year. A selection of those currently available are listed below. For latest catalogue please contact Frith Book Co.

Town Books 96pp, 100 photos. County and Themed Books 128pp, 150 photos (unless specified). All titles hardback laminated case and jacket except those indicated pb (paperback)

Around Bakewell	1-85937-113-2	£12.99		Around Great Yarmouth	1-85937-085-3	£12.99
Around Barnstaple	1-85937-084-5	£12.99		Around Guildford	1-85937-117-5	£12.99
Around Bath	1-85937-097-7	£12.99		Hampshire	1-85937-064-0	£14.99
Berkshire (pb)	1-85937-191-4	£9.99		Around Harrogate	1-85937-112-4	£12.99
Around Blackpool	1-85937-049-7	£12.99		Around Horsham	1-85937-127-2	£12.99
Around Bognor Regis	1-85937-055-1	£12.99		Around Ipswich	1-85937-133-7	£12.99
Around Bournemouth	1-85937-067-5	£12.99		Ireland (pb)	1-85937-181-7	£9.99
Brighton (pb)	1-85937-192-2	£8.99		Isle of Man	1-85937-065-9	£14.99
British Life A Century Ago	1-85937-103-5	£17.99		Isle of Wight	1-85937-114-0	£14.99
Buckinghamshire (pb)	1-85937-200-7	£9.99		Kent (pb)	1-85937-189-2	£9.99
Around Cambridge	1-85937-092-6	£12.99		Around Leicester	1-85937-073-x	£12.99
Cambridgeshire	1-85937-086-1	£14.99		Leicestershire (pb)	1-85937-185-x	£9.99
Canals and Waterways	1-85937-129-9	£17.99		Around Lincoln	1-85937-111-6	£12.99
Cheshire	1-85937-045-4	£14.99		Lincolnshire	1-85937-135-3	£14.99
Around Chester	1-85937-090-x	£12.99		London (pb)	1-85937-183-3	£9.99
Around Chichester	1-85937-089-6	£12.99		Around Maidstone	1-85937-056-x	£12.99
Churches of Berkshire	1-85937-170-1	£17.99		New Forest	1-85937-128-0	£14.99
Churches of Dorset	1-85937-172-8	£17.99		Around Newark	1-85937-105-1	£12.99
Colchester (pb)	1-85937-188-4	£8.99		Around Newquay	1-85937-140-x	£12.99
Cornwall	1-85937-054-3	£14.99		North Devon Coast	1-85937-146-9	£14.99
Cumbria	1-85937-101-9	£14.99		Northumberland and Tyne & Wear		
Dartmoor	1-85937-145-0	£14.99			1-85937-072-1	£14.99
Around Derby	1-85937-046-2	£12.99		Norwich (pb)	1-85937-194-9	£8.99
Derbyshire (pb)	1-85937-196-5	£9.99		Around Nottingham	1-85937-060-8	£12.99
Devon	1-85937-052-7	£14.99		Nottinghamshire (pb)	1-85937-187-6	£9.99
Dorset	1-85937-075-6	£14.99		Around Oxford	1-85937-096-9	£12.99
Dorset Coast	1-85937-062-4	£14.99		Oxfordshire	1-85937-076-4	£14.99
Down the Severn	1-85937-118-3	£14.99		Peak District	1-85937-100-0	£14.99
Down the Thames	1-85937-121-3	£14.99		Around Penzance	1-85937-069-1	£12.99
Around Dublin	1-85937-058-6	£12.99		Around Plymouth	1-85937-119-1	£12.99
East Sussex	1-85937-130-2	£14.99		Around St Ives	1-85937-068-3	£12.99
Around Eastbourne	1-85937-061-6	£12.99		Around Scarborough	1-85937-104-3	£12.99
Edinburgh (pb)	1-85937-193-0	£8.99		Scotland (pb)	1-85937-182-5	£9.99
English Castles	1-85937-078-0	£14.99		Scottish Castles	1-85937-077-2	£14.99
Essex	1-85937-082-9	£14.99		Around Sevenoaks and Tonbridge		
Around Exeter	1-85937-126-4	£12.99			1-85937-057-8	£12.99
Exmoor	1-85937-132-9	£14.99		Around Southampton	1-85937-088-8	£12.99
Around Falmouth	1-85937-066-7	£12.99		Around Southport	1-85937-106-x	£12.99

Available from your local bookshop or from the publisher

Frith Book Co Titles (continued)

Scottish Castles	1-85937-077-2	£14.99		Around Torbay	1-85937-063-2	£12.99
Around Sevenoaks and Tonbridge	1-85937-057-8	£12.99		Around Truro	1-85937-147-7	£12.99
Around Southampton	1-85937-088-8	£12.99		Victorian & Edwardian Kent	1-85937-149-3	£14.99
Around Southport	1-85937-106-x	£12.99		Victorian & Edwardian Maritime Album		
Around Shrewsbury	1-85937-110-8	£12.99			1-85937-144-2	£17.99
Shropshire	1-85937-083-7	£14.99		Victorian & Edwardian Yorkshire	1-85937-154-x	£14.99
South Devon Coast	1-85937-107-8	£14.99		Victorian Seaside	1-85937-159-0	£17.99
South Devon Living Memories	1-85937-168-x	£14.99		Warwickshire (pb)	1-85937-203-1	£9.99
Staffordshire (96pp)	1-85937-047-0	£12.99		Welsh Castles	1-85937-120-5	£14.99
Stone Circles & Ancient Monuments				West Midlands	1-85937-109-4	£14.99
	1-85937-143-4	£17.99		West Sussex	1-85937-148-5	£14.99
Around Stratford upon Avon	1-85937-098-5	£12.99		Wiltshire	1-85937-053-5	£14.99
Sussex (pb)	1-85937-184-1	£9.99		Around Winchester	1-85937-139-6	£12.99

Frith Book Co titles available Autumn 2000

Cotswolds (pb)	1-85937-230-9	£9.99	Sep		English Country Houses	1-85937-161-2	£17.99	Oct
Cornish Coast	1-85937-163-9	£14.99	Sep		Folkestone (pb)	1-85937-124-8	£9.99	Oct
County Durham	1-85937-123-x	£14.99	Sep		Humberside	1-85937-215-5	£14.99	Oct
Dorset Living Memories	1-85937-210-4	£14.99	Sep		Manchester (pb)	1-85937-198-1	£9.99	Oct
Dublin (pb)	1-85937-231-7	£9.99	Sep		Norfolk Living Memories	1-85937-217-1	£14.99	Oct
Herefordshire	1-85937-174-4	£14.99	Sep		Preston (pb)	1-85937-212-0	£9.99	Oct
Kent Living Memories	1-85937-125-6	£14.99	Sep		Reading (pb)	1-85937-238-4	£9.99	Oct
Leeds (pb)	1-85937-202-3	£9.99	Sep		Salisbury (pb)	1-85937-239-2	£9.99	Oct
Ludlow (pb)	1-85937-176-0	£9.99	Sep		South Hams	1-85937-220-1	£14.99	Oct
Norfolk (pb)	1-85937-195-7	£9.99	Sep		Suffolk (pb)	1-85937-221-x	£9.99	Oct
North Yorks (pb)	1-85937-236-8	£9.99	Sep		Swansea (pb)	1-85937-167-1	£9.99	Oct
Somerset	1-85937-153-1	£14.99	Sep		West Yorkshire (pb)	1-85937-201-5	£9.99	Oct
Surrey (pb)	1-85937-240-6	£9.99	Sep					
Tees Valley & Cleveland	1-85937-211-2	£14.99	Sep		Around Aylesbury (pb)	1-85937-227-9	£9.99	Nov
Thanet (pb)	1-85937-116-7	£9.99	Sep		Around Bradford (pb)	1-85937-204-x	£9.99	Nov
Tiverton (pb)	1-85937-178-7	£9.99	Sep		Around Chichester (pb)	1-85937-228-7	£9.99	Nov
Victorian and Edwardian Sussex					East Anglia (pb)	1-85937-265-1	£9.99	Nov
	1-85937-157-4	£14.99	Sep		East London	1-85937-080-2	£14.99	Nov
Weymouth (pb)	1-85937-209-0	£9.99	Sep		Gloucestershire	1-85937-102-7	£14.99	Nov
Worcestershire	1-85937-152-3	£14.99	Sep		Greater Manchester (pb)	1-85937-266-x	£9.99	Nov
Yorkshire Living Memories	1-85937-166-3	£14.99	Sep		Hastings & Bexhill (pb)	1-85937-131-0	£9.99	Nov
					Helston (pb)	1-85937-214-7	£9.99	Nov
British Life A Century Ago (pb)					Lancaster, Morecombe & Heysham (pb)			
	1-85937-213-9	£9.99	Oct			1-85937-233-3	£9.99	Nov
Camberley (pb)	1-85937-222-8	£9.99	Oct		Peterborough (pb)	1-85937-219-8	£9.99	Nov
Cardiff (pb)	1-85937-093-4	£9.99	Oct		Piers	1-85937-237-6	£17.99	Nov
Carmarthenshire	1-85937-216-3	£14.99	Oct		Wiltshire Living Memories	1-85937-245-7	£14.99	Nov
Cheltenham (pb)	1-85937-095-0	£9.99	Oct		Windmills & Watermills	1-85937-242-2	£17.99	Nov
Cornwall (pb)	1-85937-229-5	£9.99	Oct		York (pb)	1-85937-199-x	£9.99	Nov

See Frith books on the internet www.frithbook.co.uk

FRITH PRODUCTS & SERVICES

Francis Frith would doubtless be pleased to know that the pioneering publishing venture he started in 1860 still continues today. A hundred and forty years later, The Francis Frith Collection continues in the same innovative tradition and is now one of the foremost publishers of vintage photographs in the world. Some of the current activities include:

Interior Decoration

Today Frith's photographs can be seen framed and as giant wall murals in thousands of pubs, restaurants, hotels, banks, retail stores and other public buildings throughout the country. In every case they enhance the unique local atmosphere of the places they depict and provide reminders of gentler days in an increasingly busy and frenetic world.

Product Promotions

Frith products are used by many major companies to promote the sales of their own products or to reinforce their own history and heritage. Frith promotions have been used by Hovis bread, Courage beers, Scots Porage Oats, Colman's mustard, Cadbury's foods, Mellow Birds coffee, Dunhill pipe tobacco, Guinness, and Bulmer's Cider.

Genealogy and Family History

As the interest in family history and roots grows world-wide, more and more people are turning to Frith's photographs of Great Britain for images of the towns, villages and streets where their ancestors lived; and, of course, photographs of the churches and chapels where their ancestors were christened, married and buried are an essential part of every genealogy tree and family album.

Frith Products

All Frith photographs are available Framed or just as Mounted Prints and Posters (size 23 x 16 inches). These may be ordered from the address below. From time to time other products - Address Books, Calendars, Table Mats, etc - are available.

The Internet

Already twenty thousand Frith photographs can be viewed and purchased on the internet. By the end of the year 2000 some 60,000 Frith photographs will be available on the internet. The number of sites is constantly expanding, each focussing on different products and services from the Collection.
The main Frith sites are listed below.
www.francisfrith.co.uk
www.frithbook.co.uk

See the complete list of Frith Books at:
www.frithbook.co.uk
This web site is regularly updated with the latest list of publications from the Frith Book Company. If you wish to buy books relating to another part of the country that your local bookshop does not stock, you may purchase on-line.

For further information, trade, or author enquiries please contact us at the address below:
The Francis Frith Collection, Frith's Barn, Teffont, Salisbury, Wiltshire, England SP3 5QP.
Tel: +44 (0)1722 716 376 Fax: +44 (0)1722 716 881   Email: uksales@francisfrith.co.uk

See Frith books on the internet www.frithbook.co.uk

TO RECEIVE YOUR FREE MOUNTED PRINT

Mounted Print
Overall size 14 x 11 inches

Cut out this Voucher and return it with your remittance for £1.50 to cover postage and handling, to UK addresses. For overseas addresses please include £4.00 post and handling. Choose any photograph included in this book. Your SEPIA print will be A4 in size, and mounted in a cream mount with burgundy rule lines, overall size 14 x 11 inches.

Order additional Mounted Prints at HALF PRICE (only £7.49 each*)

If there are further pictures you would like to order, possibly as gifts for friends and family, purchase them at half price (no additional postage and handling required).

Have your Mounted Prints framed*

For an additional £14.95 per print you can have your chosen Mounted Print framed in an elegant polished wood and gilt moulding, overall size 16 x 13 inches (no additional postage and handling required).

> *** IMPORTANT!**
> These special prices are only available if ordered using the original voucher on this page (no copies permitted) and at the same time as your free Mounted Print, for delivery to the same address

Frith Collectors' Guild

From time to time we publish a magazine of news and stories about Frith photographs and further special offers of Frith products. If you would like 12 months FREE membership, please return this form.

Send completed forms to:
The Francis Frith Collection, Frith's Barn, Teffont, Salisbury, Wiltshire SP3 5QP

Voucher for **FREE** and Reduced Price Frith Prints

Picture no.	Page number	Qty	Mounted @ £7.49	Framed + £14.95	Total Cost
		1	**Free of charge***	£	£
			£7.49	£	£
			£7.49	£	£
			£7.49	£	£
			£7.49	£	£
			£7.49	£	£

Please allow 28 days for delivery	*** Post & handling**	**£1.50**
Book Title	**Total Order Cost**	**£**

Please do not photocopy this voucher. Only the original is valid, so please cut it out and return it to us.

I enclose a cheque / postal order for £ . . . . made payable to 'The Francis Frith Collection' OR please debit my Mastercard / Visa / Switch / Amex card *(credit cards please on all overseas orders)*

Number . . . .

Issue No(Switch only) . . . . .Valid from (Amex/Switch) . . . .

Expires . . . . Signature . . . .

Name Mr/Mrs/Ms . . . .

Address . . . .

. . . .

. . . .

. . . . Postcode . . . .

Daytime Tel No . . . .   Valid to 31/12/02

The Francis Frith Collectors' Guild

Please enrol me as a member for 12 months free of charge.

Name Mr/Mrs/Ms . . . .

Address . . . .

. . . .

. . . .

. . . . Postcode . . . .

Free Print - see overleaf